Love Overcomes All Barriers

CW00794283

Aldivan Torres

Love Overcomes All Barriers

_____

Author: Aldivan Torres

©2023- Aldivan Torres

All rights reserved.

Series: Spirituality and self-help

_____

_____

Aldivan Torres, born in Brazil, is a well-established writer in several genres. To date, it has published titles in dozens of languages. From an early age, he has always been a lover of the art of writing, having consolidated a professional career from the second half of 2013. With his writings, he hopes to contribute to the culture of Pernambuco and Brazil, awakening the pleasure of reading in those who do not yet have the habit.

Dedication

This is my fiftieth book. I dedicate it first of all to God, for whom everything lives. I dedicate it to my mother, my family, my readers, my supporters, and those who encourage literature in general.

Let's build a country with more education, more health, more justice, and more love among all. Let's build now a country of the present and the future. May the culture of Brazil be increasingly admired and respected all over the world.

About the book

This book is more of an immersion in divine and world wisdom. Their reflections fill us with wisdom, making us reflect and apply their good practices. More than a book, it is a guide to wisdom, religiosity, and well-being.

The book invites all readers who enjoy good literature. We will learn more and more to be ethical, loving, caring and generous human beings with others. The world needs the disciples of goodness and their good works to become a better place to live. Support an independent writer. Support the children's literature. Contribute so that he can make a living from his art.

Love Overcomes All Barriers

We all have free will. There is no point in blaming God for the wars in the world

Don't make rash decisions

Have your own originality

Be faithful in the little things. And you will have the confidence to be faithful in great things

If others reject you, you respond with your value

Being weak is also a virtue

Knowing how to choose your boyfriend is a great gift

Remigius of Reims

Choosing as a bishop

In attendance at the project

Conversation with King Childeric

The Conversion of Clovis

Final summary

Is it good for you to evaluate yourself?

Is it normal to have a new relationship right after another relationship ends?

Who should we marry?

What is the Brazilian private school like?

Black students still have little opportunity to pursue higher education

Why do we want the world to pay attention to us?

After a girl becomes a mother, her friends are her children

How hard it is to date these days

We have to respect mothers, because they have stories to tell

Parents should not compel the love of their children. They must give free love.

We should never gossip about other people's lives, especially when it harms others.

Dreams of love are beautiful, but it's better to fall into reality

How to deal with a rebellious thirteen-year-old teenager?

There is no point in picking fights or cultivating hatred

If someone complains in a relationship, it's a sign that they're falling apart

Why do you reject your husband?

How bad it is to date someone who corrects you all the time

The man who does not keep his promises is not to be trusted

When you dispense with leisure, it's easy to save money

To be able to work in a company, the employee has to have team spirit

To be a good worker, you need to be okay with yourself

What do we learn from the dark nights of our lives?

Is having many relationships a sign of love happiness?

Why don't relationships last forever?

Dutchman's Stone

Girl's Stone

The Horse Graveyard

Why do many artists regret being famous?

Why shouldn't we be afraid?

We are complete people. So avoid the lack

Did you know that death is inevitable?

What do you think of old age?

Don't want to control other people's lives

How to get along well as a family

The story of Afonso Pena

Going to visit the tomato plantation

In the Gold Mine

Family Reunion

A Debate in Law School

Afonso Pena's political career

Remember your origins

A beautiful story of overcoming challenges

How much maturity has changed me

How do you see a lover?

The Story of Two Lovers

Can men and women be friends?

The love between friends turned into a relationship

There are men who live double lives

Don't be depressed

My personal story as an example of overcoming challenges

You don't need anyone's support to win

The Little Gymnast

Don't play hard in a relationship

To be mature is to take random conversations for granted

Forgiveness

Jesus' forgiveness of the prostitute

We've got to learn to like ourselves

Don't judge anyone in your personal battle

What does God require of us?

Faith and Hope

What does it mean to be romantic?

A new beginning

It was October 22, 2023. As usual, I wake up around eight o'clock in the morning. I get up, leave my room, and go to the kitchen. There, I meet my sister who had already prepared breakfast. I sit down in a chair around the table and start eating bread and coffee. It was what was available, and I was happy to be there. I had been working from home for four years and I missed the routine of going to work every morning and coming back in the afternoon. But why had I chosen remote work? I chose this type of work because of two main factors: forgetting Brian, my great love at work, and because of the difficulty of getting around if I had to attend every day in person. So taking refuge in remote work was my best option.

Dalva

There's someone calling you. It looks like it's your fellow adventurer.

Godlike

Tell him to come in and make himself comfortable.

Dalva

Sure. I'm going to call him.

Moments later, Renato's silhouette appears in front of me. How beautiful he looked. It had been about three years since we had any lasting adventures, and that was a great sin for our literature. But he was there, with a very special look on his face, and it made me tremble with anxiety.

Godlike

My dear Renato, how are you?

Renato

I'm doing very well. What about you?

Godlike

In the routine of remote work for about four years. This has distressed me and demotivated me as well. I miss our great adventures around the world. Tell me, what's new?

Renato

My mom wants to see you. She needs to talk to you about it. Could you accompany me to the top of the mountain?

Godlike

That would be great. I'm going to ask my boss for a month's vacation. Only then will I be able to accompany you.

Renato

OK. I'll wait for you to call your boss.

Divino got up from the table, pulled out his cell phone, and immediately called his boss. In a nutshell, he explained his urgent appointments and was assured of being taken care of. Then he hung up his phone and came back to the table with a smile on his face.

Godlike

I just got cleared by my boss. I'm going to pack my bags and we're off to the top of the mountain. Wait about ten minutes and I'll pack my bags.

Renato

Make yourself comfortable, dear. I might even wait a little longer. I know things don't magically solve themselves.

Divino got up from the table and with a few steps, crossed the corridor, and reached his room. It was by choosing the most necessary items that could lead to this magical journey that promised great things. About twenty minutes later, the suitcase was packed and he was reunited with Renato. Together, they leave the house and begin to climb the mountain of Ororubá, the so-called sacred mountain.

The ascent of the mountain

The pair of adventurers began to climb the mountain on the chosen trail. Step by step, they were going to begin a great enterprise towards the top of the mountain as they had twelve years ago. What has changed since then? At the time, the divine little one was just a boy and Renato was still a child. Together, they were inexperienced about any knowledge that life could teach them. Now, another decade later, the tables had changed: Divino was a mature adult while his companion in adventures was a young man full of dreams. They already had a great cultural background, but they wanted to learn more and more in order to evolve on their path as apprentices. And along with them, all readers would go in search of getting to know new worlds, living adventures, experiencing diverse situations that they never thought of reflecting. But continuously all of us would have this opportunity for reflection throughout his trajectory.

They complete a quarter of the route and promote the first stop of the walk. Divino opens his backpack and shares bread and crackers with his companion. As they eat, they start a dialogue.

Renato

And what have you done in these three years that we have not had lasting contact?

Godlike

I ended an important cycle which was to leave face-to-face work and started working remotely in my government job. Today, it's been ten years since I've been in public service.

Renato

Congratulations, Divine. I know how important this was to his trajectory. But why did you decide to work remotely? What led you to decide that?

Godlike

A love of work and the difficulty of locomotion. I had been in love with Brian, who is a co-worker, for eight years. This feeling, despite being very beautiful, made me feel very bad because I was not reciprocated. So leaving face-to-face work to go to remote work took me out of his daily life and made me forget about him. I was sure he didn't love me. Simply, Brian never visited me at my home even after four years of remote work. If a person loves you, they would never act that way. So I discarded Brian from the love possibilities of my life. I feel better. I feel happy and without suffering. Another issue that I also took into account was to stop using public transport every day. In addition to the risk of an accident, I waited a long time for the transport to fill up and this made me upset. It was something that tired me a lot. So remote work was really good in that sense. What about you? How are you?

Renato

I finished college and got a job as an administrative assistant in the city. Now, I'm a man with responsibilities.

Godlike

When are you getting married?

Renato

I'm like you: I don't want commitment. I understood that being free, life is much more enjoyed. I'm in no hurry to get married. I don't think I was born for this. I like partying, having fun, but no commitment.

Godlike

You're completely right, dear friend. I'm not getting married either. I want to discover all that life has to offer. I count on your company for that.

Renato

Clear. It will be a great pleasure to accompany you on this great journey. It's time for us to get back on track. Let's go together?

Godlike

Of course. Right now.

The walk continued. A strong wind blows, rattling the visitors. An inner fear consumed them, but it did not stop them on the way up. They knew that this act was a release from all the uncertainties that surrounded them. Nothing else mattered at that moment and they felt lonely in the act of walking. Shortly after, they complete half of the proposed route.

From now on, they focus only on walking, which was a huge task to be accomplished. How happy would they be when they completed the journey? They weren't sure if Nothing, but they followed their adventurous instinct for hours on end. Soon they would know of an unforeseeable outcome.

Finally they get to the top. Continuing on the trail, they go to the house of the guardian of the mountain. Perhaps they would find some answers there. When they arrive at the house, they knock on the door, are answered and settle on a sofa. An old acquaintance introduces himself.

Flower

How are you, my dear Divine? How long has it been, hasn't it?

Godlike

I am fine. What good news do they bring you?

Flower

I was invited to be a model in Paris. I'm excited and hesitant. I'm afraid, but I also really wanted to get to know this life abroad. What do you think?

Godlike

It's really anyone's guess, isn't it, Renato? There are so many haunting stories that I can't even tell you.

Renato

That's that. That's when we thought we could help this friend. How about if we all went to Paris and spent our holidays there?

Mountain Guardian

It would only be thirty days of vacation. We would take the opportunity to get to know the best places in Paris. It would all be very advantageous for all of us.

Godlike

OK. I've already packed my bags. May Paris await us.

Everyone applauds the decision and goes to pack their bags. It would be a great adventure in France, one of the great European countries.

Museum d'Orsay

The group was in the second most important museum in Paris. There are several works of art in a very cozy atmosphere for tourists.

Godlike

What did we learn about art here? We learn to admire the work of each artist who shows us their world.

Flower

It reminds me of my first client from Paris. In addition to modeling, I'm being a luxury escort to be able to pay the bills. His name was Peter. We hung out a few times together and he was extremely courteous. It is considered a good sweet wine from Paris.

Renato

There's always a problem on these tours. But if you're happy, who are we to criticize you?

Mountain Guardian

Generally, the LGBTI group needs to prostitute themselves in order to survive in these havens. Nothing unusual. The good thing is the museum. Pure beauty and unparalleled culture.

Godlike

Yes. Respecting these events and moments is special. And we are here to support you, dear Little Flower. Keep telling us about your love adventures. We'd love to hear from you.

Flower

Thank you, dear. I loved the tour as one of the best I've ever had. Let's go to the next tour.

Eiffel Tower

The group was in a restaurant in front of the Eiffel Tower. They felt free and free to talk for a while.

Godlike

Seeing it from here, how wonderful this tower is. It is truly a privilege to participate in this journey. How do you feel, little flower?

Flower

I was remembering my last love affair. He was a great master like the richness of the art of this tower. France is truly a special country.

Renato

And how special French women are, too. In fact, this country is special and breathes culture.

Mountain Guardian

The tower can represent the emotional balance we have in the face of life. If we exaggerate one part, we will surely lose the direction of life. The secret to doing well is to try a little bit of everything, in moderation. It is perhaps a crucial decision that awaits us. If we know how to make the best decision, we can be happy in life.

Godlike

The tower guides us to enjoy this night with a lot of liveliness. May we live today without worrying about what the future holds. Let's be happy now!

Flower

And that we are happy with our specificities. May everyone have the right to be happy, regardless of race, creed, gender or religion.

The night progresses and our friends stay in that restaurant eating and drinking well. It was another chapter of wonderful Paris.

Godlike

Loved the museum exhibit. It's like I'm inside the world culture, so rich is the museum.

Renato

Every photo we took was magnificent. It is an unforgettable place that will remain in our hearts.

Flower

The Louvre Museum is yet another facet of Paris. We felt at ease, as if I was with one of the best friends. Simply charming.

Mountain Guardian

This visit was a great event in our lives. With the culture of the museum, in the feelings prepared to explore Paris, the great capital of France.

After a full day of sightseeing, the group bids farewell to the museum and returns home. The upcoming events were eagerly guarded by all.

The cathedral of Notre-Dame is fantastic and holds a lot of history. An invitation to get to know French culture.

Godlike

A story told even by the writers. It is a dive into world history through wonderful sensations.

Flower

This place refers to history. This place refers to reflection, society and decisions. It's a big page of history.

Mountain Guardian

We remember movies and books about this monument. We remember our own memories of this colossal experience. Very good to be here.

Renato

Our youthful spirit meets the French past and that's a bit unsettling. It's a little hard to deal with those emotions. But when we realize that the magic is in ourselves, we feel liberated to love and live.

It was a very fruitful day where they had the good fortune to face this historical monument. And they would move on to the next goal with more happiness, anxiety, and excitement. I'm glad they were living through all of this.

Final Summary

Little Flower found happiness abroad. She lived her life as if she had never had the opportunity to be who she was. With all the difficulties, I recognized the help of Divino in this whole process. For a world with more freedom, tolerance and love for people.

This process of knowledge heals us

What is life? What is the meaning of life, of loving and relating? What is the point of seeking fulfillment in our lives? Is it killing this lack that suffocates us? There are many and diverse factors that lead us to relate to someone and believe that this is the right thing to do.

We live this process of self-knowledge in a broad way throughout life. We live the pain of failures, the joy of achievements, we live the pleasure of relationships, and in an intuitive way, we live our frustrations with our heads held high. Perhaps what we seek in the other is not so much complementarity. Maybe we seek the answers to so many things that we seek and see it as meaningless. Perhaps it is knowledge and wisdom that guides us at every step of evolution in this world.

This process of knowledge heals and transforms us. It is a liberation to understand that we are independent and that our boyfriend, fiancé or partner is not responsible for this inner feeling that we have that we call happiness. So maybe dating someone is a physical, psychological, and human need. But never, under any circumstances, a dependence on external happiness. Therefore, I say: married or single, happiness is your own construction.

Don't let other people's gazes affect you

Don't give in to the opinions of others. Those who criticize you only want to see the worst of you. Do your own will, even if it has bad consequences. It is by living and learning that one is truly happy. Take your own course with grit, strength and courage. Make your story count.

Don't let a failed marriage hold you back

If your partner treats you badly in any way and if you stay in the marriage due to financial dependence or your children, I tell you: it's not worth it. It pays to be okay with yourself, to have your job, to have your financial independence, to be free and to be happy. If something hurts you, push it away.

The end of a marriage is not the end of the world. It's just the beginning of a new time where you'll seek personal improvement. It's an opening to new possibilities, where you can find your true happiness. Maybe it all goes wrong again but if you don't try, you'll never know. So keep pushing until you get it.

When someone doesn't value us

When someone doesn't value us, it's an open wound and a pain that never ends. But to break this perverse cycle of addiction, we must experience new situations in our life. We must experience the greatness of our one's own being through continual meditation and reflection.

When someone doesn't value us, it's necessary to overcome rejection and surrender to God's great love that covers us all. It takes faith to find ourselves with an inner strength that only we know. And yes, this power of the universe can completely transform us.

When we love, we always want to be together with the person we love

When loving a person, we always want to be together, sharing amazing moments with them. This lasting contact is not always possible. Sometimes we have many obligations that distance us from our loved one. But when it's time to meet the person again, our happiness quickly returns.

Together, we can live big and small moments. But for those who are single like me, life goes by quickly without much news. Being single, we have fewer obligations and fewer problems to occupy ourselves. It's a relief to know that we only depend on ourselves.

Being together is not always a sign of good friendship. Sometimes the worst demons come to torment us in our own home. So it's the person's actions that show us what they really are. Observe this and go about your life without any major worries.

If someone proposes to contribute to you, then don't treat them badly

If someone has helped you at any unfavorable time in your life, be grateful for it. Never belittle the action or the author of the transformation in your life. Ungrateful people are the worst people we can meet in life. These are people who don't remember the past and how much they needed us.

Repay the good you've received even if the other person doesn't need it. Make your actions great moments of charity, love and altruism. Make your mark on the world as long as you can live and share good times. Long live love, if you are allowed to do so. When you reach old age, you will have a story to tell. When you reach old age, you will remember the good times you had in life.

To maintain a healthy marriage, you need to talk and compromise a lot

A marriage is a combination of two people trying to live together in harmony. To maintain peace together, one must talk, compromise on some things, and have one's wishes fulfilled. Those who are bossy and intransigent end up being alone. Those who are only interested in money don't have a happy life either.

Is it worth keeping a marriage? For those who want to have a family, the marriage issue can be a good one. But for those who want to have their freedom in the first place, maybe being single is the best option. If you are single, you can go out with multiple partners without giving any explanation. Those who are single have fewer obligations to potential offspring. So it's a case to think about.

It's good to be financially and emotionally independent

Never let your livelihood be dependent on other people. It's humiliating to beg for alms from anyone in order to survive. If you're young, go for it. It's so beautiful to work and conquer your stuff with your sweat. It is so beautiful to contribute to society by being an employee who fulfills his obligations.

Having emotional and financial independence is a great blessing. It's feeling good, free, and powerful. It's making sure you'll be okay despite your misfortunes. So it's our best achievement ever.

Try to have a good relationship with your partner's family members. It is the least that can be expected from a lasting and beneficial relationship. If you don't like any of them, rethink your decision to marry. As much as your partner likes you, they will always be by their family's side, so don't ask them to choose.

Attend family gatherings and always be kind and polite. Show your best side and try to talk to everyone in a friendly way. It is in these moments that you will have the opportunity to better get along with all of them.

Know when and how to act to please your partner. You don't have to give him full-time attention, but whenever possible, be with him helping his work with a smile on your face. It is companionship that marks a relationship and transforms it into a great paradise. Go ahead with your plans and projects, you are able to accomplish them all.

Who hasn't loved in their life? Who hasn't suffered for love? Who hasn't wanted to have a happy marriage? If you answered affirmatively to any of these questions, then you are a sensitive person.

We've all had a past life love. Perhaps a love that was not fulfilled. They both traveled back in time and met again in this life. And Sometimes they fulfill that desire to be together. To be happy together. But sometimes it doesn't always last long. Sometimes true love doesn't last more than three years. Sometimes it's just a beautiful learning about what life is all about. And when you finish that experiment, you're completely fulfilled.

Those who have never allowed themselves to love will never know what a past-life love is. It's simply looking at the other and having an inexplicable feeling of love, affection and attraction. It's just magical to understand love at work in our lives. The best answer to this lies in ourselves and what we consider important for our well-being. If you've found love, enjoy it while there's still time. May they be happy as long as there is love.

Maybe love doesn't work for us because we don't have an affinity with anyone

We are complex human beings. We have a complex mind. And maybe that's why you don't work out with anyone. As others have different perceptions and affinities than yours, so it doesn't take the minimum for you to maintain a relationship. And think about how complicated it is to have a romantic relationship these days. They are financial obligations, they are obligations to share goods, the materialism of things, our responsibilities fill our lives, we have little time to enjoy each other's company.

Maybe love doesn't work for us because we have a mental vibration that doesn't attract the right person. And is there really such a thing as the right person? More or less. There are people with more or less affinity, but never perfect. No matter how much you like someone, there will always be something that displeases you. And then it will be up to you to decide if living with this person is going to be beneficial for you.

Maybe love didn't come into your life because you just didn't allow it. Due to previous frustrations, you've blocked love in your life. You just don't even try to get to know the other person because you're full of distrust. I understand you. The fear of suffering again freezes you. The fear of giving oneself away and not being reciprocated is greater. But if you understood that people are not the same, then you would always be open to love and try to be happy countless times. yes, love is really complex.

The will to change alone is not enough

Sometimes you're not satisfied with yourself. Sometimes there's something about you that bothers you. But you haven't taken action in years for convenience. Then it's time to take action and bring more happiness into your life. Try to go out, read, travel, and have fun. Try to be an active part of life. Give your best version of yourself.

Don't just stick to the promise. Think that there are many people who depend on you. So strive to become someone better for yourself and everyone around you. You will have your good happiness in knowing that you have evolved and contributed to a more just, supportive and pleasurable world.

We must all move forward without thinking about the worst

Life is a great challenge for all of us. And thinking about life's problems can affect us hard. Think less about the problems. Live life with joy, enjoy the moments because they are unique.

If they thought the worst all the time, our lives would be a great stress. So let's walk every step to better reflect on our projects. Go in search of your dreams, carefully.

We must all move forward. We should all carry the faith we have within us and hope for the best in life. Even if the worst happens, we must be prepared for any eventuality. Then life goes on without further explanation. Just feel that pleasure of living flow into your chest. You can, should, and deserve to be happy.

Most people dream of a happy marriage and beautiful children to raise. That is their happiness. But your happiness can also be single. What we can't create is a standard of happiness that everyone follows. No one is the same as the others. Everyone has their own fears, traumas, and specificities.

Our happiness may be living alone, far away, on an island, or even on a farm. It can be working or simply spending time playing. Everyone is happy according to what they deserve. So don't envy anyone's happiness. Each of us has our own special glow.

There are two ongoing wars in the world: the war between Ukraine and Russia and the war between Israel and Palestine. Without going into the merits of the question of wars, the responsibility for wars lies with the human being himself. God has given the planet into our hands. So don't blame God for the actions of human beings. We are the real culprits.

The world has to learn to cultivate peace and abolish wars. The world has to learn love, forgiveness, charity and generosity. We have to make a difference in the world by planting the seeds of good. Be good in your attitudes towards yourself and others.

Hatred and anger are bad counselors. It is very sensible to let the situation get more comfortable and only then make a definitive decision. When we coldly analyze the issue, we can have a correct thought about what to actually do in each question. And sometimes the best solution is exactly the opposite of what you were thinking.

Practice forgiveness and mercy. Do good without looking at whom. Raise the flag of peace, altruism and understanding. What makes it possible for you to be happy is exactly to do good to others. The good we do will do more good for ourselves than for others. Think about it fondly.

Have your own originality

Be who you truly are. Don't be put off by other people's opinions. When we get carried away with what others want, it will cause us a big problem. As much as it hurts your reality, be yourself in any situation.

But it is quite true that we often give in to societal pressure out of fear. Sometimes we don't have a way out and we start to live a character. It destroys our psyche. What we must deal with is the fear of acceptance and this has to be a joint attitude with the family.

If pleasing others is necessary, as is my case, then all that remains is regret. It is a life that is lost for a long time. In my case, there's no point in even talking because my siblings are closed-minded. So to live with them, I have to be submissive. It invalidates any kind of love I may have. That's the saddest thing about my trajectory. Maybe one day I can break free from all of this. So I hope.

Be faithful in the little things. And you will have the confidence to be faithful in great things

We get to know friends in the little troubles. If someone abandons you to your fate, then you are not trustworthy. Follow the side of true friends, those who care about you. But don't be fooled. Such friends are rare.

Cultivate good friendships because it's worth more than money. Cultivate good relationships because they make things easier for us. Who has never had to solve something at the bank and by knowledge did not have their problem solved quickly? That's that. Here's proof that good relationships bear fruit.

The faithful friend is the one who supports you in the best and worst times. It is at these times that we realize who is really by our side. But don't be sad if you're alone. God never abandons us in any situation. Truly, God is everyone's best friend.

If others reject you, you respond with your value

There were more than ten thousand professional and love rejections. But that didn't destroy me. I have found in myself my true love, for I put myself first. I have also developed my religiosity and I see God at work in my life, loving me as a son. I am so grateful for all that God has given me.

So thank those who rejected you. Be thankful, then, that you have gotten rid of a problem. You can live without love. You just can't live without God, health, or money. But without love you can survive. I thank you for valuing yourself and seeing that your happiness depends only on you and no one else. A leader of himself is emotionally balanced, knows how to act, and has the best plans for the future. Be the best version of yourself.

Being weak is also a virtue

' No one is strong all the time. We all have a moment of weakness where we need other people's support. And there's no shame in being dependent on that help. Sometimes our failure is so great that we find ourselves torn apart. Then we must rise from the rubble and be born again.

In God, we find the strength we need to move forward with faith toward our goals. Yes, it is possible to achieve our dreams with hard work, dedication and love for others. So let's lift our spirits and move forward with a lot of race. You're already a big winner.

Knowing how to choose your boyfriend is a great gift

Be selective with your boyfriends. Date someone you like, who has a sexual affinity, and someone who completes you spiritually. Money is not so important in this case. Although people only relate to people of the same financial standard, I would say that this is a big loss. There are bricklayers, cleaners, manual laborers, who could be great husbands but who have no chance of finding someone.

As for getting married, think carefully about whether you really want that for your life. Getting married is a big responsibility and can be a big problem if we marry the wrong person. It can be a resounding financial and sentimental loss. So be very careful in your sentimental choices.

Choosing as a bishop

Bishop

I have some beautiful news to share with you. Because of your noble talents, I have chosen you as my successor. What do you think?

Remigius

That's a big responsibility. Are you sure that a twenty-two-year-old would be capable of such a mission?

Bishop

I am convinced of that. I've been watching you for a long time, and I realize you're a prepared man. That's why, today, I'm giving you this position because I'm old and I can't work anymore.

Remigius

So I accept. Thank you so much for trusting me. I'll do my best.

Everyone applauds the choice. That was the beginning of the young man's career as bishop. May God bless your mission and your project.

In attendance at the project

Leandra

Bishop, I'm coming to ask you for advice, I'm not in a good phase.

Remigius

What's up, honey? Explain further.

Leandra

I'm having problems in my marriage. I've been having fights with my husband. Sometimes I'm the one who gets annoyed by anything. Sometimes he's the one who's always busy. We had a happy relationship. But over time it seems like that's falling apart.

Remigius

Their relationship has become routine. To overcome this, we need to innovate. Go on trips with your husband. Try new things. Try to forgive your faults. Be open to listening to your husband. Believe me, things can still be managed.

Leandra

I loved hearing from you, Father. I will apply all your advice.

Remigius

Well done, dear. Go in peace and may God be with you. You will be very happy.

Remigius fulfilled his duties as bishop, father, counselor and pastor together to the community. His reputation was as an intelligent and persuasive man. Certainly, his appointment as bishop had been the best choice of all.

Conversation with King Childeric

Childeric

To what do I owe the honor of such an illustrious visit to my castle?

Remigius

You're a good person. You are a fair king with all citizens. But all that's left is to put these false gods aside.

Childeric

I don't quite understand. I have my own gods and I like them. I wanted that to be respected.

Remigius

If you knew the great love that Jesus Christ has for us and the protection of the Blessed Virgin over the faithful, you would be astonished. It is the true love that only God can give.

Childeric

I respect your thinking, but I have another faith. I believe in other things. I will treat all Christians in the best way, but it is a pity that I do not convert. I don't feel ready for that.

Remigius

OK. I'm not going to insist. When you feel ready, just call me. I will be eagerly awaiting this achievement.

The bishop withdrew and went about his business. Sometime later, the news spread that the king had died. In the succession to the throne, his son named Clovis was elected.

The Conversion of Clovis

Remigius arranged a meeting with Clovis to pursue his goal.

Remigius

Behold, I come to proclaim the King of kings and Lord of lords. Jesus Christ was a great prophet in the Roman Empire. He is the Son of God who came down to earth to teach us the divine word. With his great teachings, Jesus showed us that he was in search of the greatest sinners. What do you say?

Clovis

How does this Jesus prove that he is the son of God?

Remigius

For the greatness of his teachings and for his miracles. Jesus turned water into wine, raised the dead, healed the blind and crippled, forgave the prostitute. Jesus thus shows that he is the God of the excluded.

Clovis

Impressive. What happened to Jesus?

Remigius

He was killed by the Jews, but rose again on the third day. He is present in the lives of all of us who believe in him. How about if you embrace that belief?

Clovis

After everything I've heard, I really believe that. How can I enter the Christian religion?

Remigius

I'm going to baptize you in the river. You will receive the holy spirit and become a member of our church.

A week later, the king and his troops were baptized by Remigius. He stood out as a great shepherd of souls, for people who were looking for a meaning to live. This was very good, because it was putting him in a prominent position.

Final summary

Remigius did a great job as a bishop. During seventy years of mission, he spread the divine word among people who did not know Christ. He also carried out charitable projects and support for those most in need. His day is celebrated on January 13 and is one of the most important saints in the Catholic Church.

Is it good for you to evaluate yourself?

The internal evaluation process makes us check defects and qualities. This is effective for correcting mistakes and getting more hits. It is a time of meditation, reflection, self-care, and self-love. You have to value yourself, put yourself first and see what's best for you.

With the right assessment, you will have a path to follow that best suits your needs. Then you will be able to make the best decisions of your life. Go ahead and be proud of who you are.

Is it normal to have a new relationship right after another relationship ends?

Yes, it's normal by today's standards. People tend to dismiss others extremely easily. It is the time when people love less and less and are selfish, arrogant, arrogant and proud. It's a material world, where it's every man for himself.

There are no rules when ending a relationship. But I would say that in the past there was more feeling and more respect for the other's story. It was a better world with people who loved and respected each other more. The teachers were respected by the students, unlike what it is today. So education, health, and civility were affected by the new times. Hopefully this will get better one day.

Who should we marry?

We should marry someone we feel good about. When you get older and all things get difficult for you, all that will be left is the company of your partner. And if you don't have love for it, you just won't stand it. Because all other things are fleeting.

But if you allow me to give my opinion, it's better to be single. Better is to have your freedom and not have to be accountable for your actions to anyone. It's not healthy to be controlled by someone else. It is not healthy to live with the burden of responsibility. It's not healthy to stop being happy to please the other. Think about it.

What is the Brazilian private school like?

The Brazilian private elementary school is much better than the public school in terms of quality. We have better teaching materials, more qualified teachers, better investment. As a result, students learn much more.

In higher education, on the other hand, public schools surpass private schools. Because they are better prepared, places in public schools are mostly occupied by wealthy students. But nowadays, we also have quotas for public school students. Whether they will be able to graduate is another story.

Nowadays, in Brazil, we have racial quotas for black students. But still, the presence of blacks in college is a rare fact. When we see a black person graduating, it becomes news. Brazil is still reaping the fruits of slavery and racial prejudice. But over time, things get better.

We must fight against prejudice in all its facets. We must fight for better health, education, the environment, and an environment with less corruption. We want a fairer country where everyone can effectively have more opportunities.

The world doesn't just revolve around you. In a relationship, there are a multitude of factors that cause our partner to disperse. This is normal and you should understand it. Expecting him to pay attention to you all the time is a bit selfish.

We always come first, in our view. But others don't see it that way. Their first place is for another object. So it's good to accept that things aren't always going to work out all the time. There will be failures that you will have to live with on a daily basis. There will be things that you wish didn't happen, but simply the unpredictable will bring it to you. This is life that is not a sea of flowers.

After a girl becomes a mother, her friends are her children

After the girl moves in with her man, everything changes. She becomes a housekeeper, takes care of the house, the children and even works outside the home. It's a very stressful routine. For a long time, the woman is isolated and has few friends to talk to. Your children become friends and confidants.

After the children grow up, the woman has more freedom. You can travel more, have fewer worries, you can do new professional qualifications, you can have more time for yourself. It is where the woman is happy again, to have a life of her own. It's great to be free and do the things you like.

How hard it is to date these days

Nowadays, it's tricky to date. Nowadays, with easy sex, people don't get attached anymore. There are also the legal and psychological issues that a relationship brings. It's a lot of a headache to be in a relationship these days.

Most people have rapid cases. Most people would rather have freedom than be attached to someone. Most people are afraid of getting hurt because they have had painful experiences in the love field. So, a lot of people end up being alone. This is a sad reality for many people.

Mothers want the best for their children. So the children should obey their mothers. As much as we think their advice is outdated, it is important for our personality building. We must respect our parents, who gave us the greatest gift of coming into the world.

If you have to choose between a partner and your family, choose your family. They are the ones who will support you when you need it most. So don't have any doubts about who loves you the most. But if you find a nice partner, also value that as a great gift.

Parents should not compel the love of their children. They must give free love.

Love is not required under any circumstances. Even parental love, which is natural, cannot be demanded. Naturally, our children will love us for our example, our character, and the education we give them. So don't worry. Your children will love you very much if you deserve it.

I had two wonderful parents who never let me lack anything. They had their faults, but they taught me a good way. Today, I am a very fulfilled person due to their influence. So that's what we should leave to our children: education and our example.

We should never gossip about other people's lives, especially when it harms others.

Do you know any secrets that would destroy someone's life? So don't tell. Telling this can disrupt a person's life and you don't have to take care of other people's lives. If others have made mistakes or are bad people, it's their problem and not yours. So minding your own business is the best medicine for that.

It has secrets that must remain guarded for the good of all. If you follow this, your chance of doing well in life is much higher. So good luck in all your endeavors.

Dreams of love are beautiful, but it's better to fall into reality

We all have Love stories to tell and many of these stories are failures, rejections, and a waste of time. When we suffer from the love we feel, it's simply not worth that love. The best option is to forget about this love and look for other possibilities. One thing is certain: even if we are alone, we have to have self-love.

Counting more than ten thousand rejections, I learned to value myself. I love myself above all, I believe in God and love for others. My only option was to be alone. As sad as it is, I feel complete and fulfilled in all my things. So I believe that a romantic love for me would just be a good complement. But I honestly don't believe in such love.

Why don't I believe in such love? Because I only see couples breaking up even though they've been married for more than ten years. Because I only see big betrayals over and over again in the best marriages. Why cheat if we love our partners so much? Why have multiple affairs even though you're happy in a relationship? I don't know how psychology defines it, but it must be something related to sex addiction, sex variety, and lack of character. But maybe it's just an unfortunate choice of the individual reflecting a great truth: he doesn't love us. Knowing and understanding this great truth can definitively rid us of all toxic relationships and focus on ourselves, on our well-being. Thinking about having you as a priority is the first step to being happy in an increasingly selfish world.

How to deal with a rebellious thirteen-year-old teenager?

With a lot of patience, it is possible to deal with this situation. Parents have an obligation to guide their children in this great phase of change. Adolescence is a major challenge in our lives. This is when we abandon childhood and go into adulthood. It is a period of great discoveries about life itself, the world, and oneself. So be very cautious with this.

Becoming a woman is very complicated for anyone. Especially in a society that is extremely demanding of women. Try to expect less from yourself and be the woman you've always dreamed of. Be the ordinary woman with big dreams and projects. Be the respectable woman who makes us proud wherever we go. Be the hero woman, but for your own family.

Nowadays, being a woman can be a great blessing as women become aware of their desires, opinions, and values. Being a woman is a challenge due to being more fragile and labeled as less competent. But don't despair. You have your inestimable value to God, to yourself, and to the world.

There is no point in picking fights or cultivating hatred

Fights and hatred only make our lives miserable. And this is what gives rise to wars and destruction in the world. I don't support violence. I think dialogue is always possible in small and large conflicts. I want a world of peace and harmony for all of us.

Try to resolve conflicts peacefully. It's a win-win for everyone. Then you'll feel good about spreading love, peace, and freedom wherever you are. May you be blessed in all your projects.

During my forty years of life, I have had several disagreements. For my part, I forgave but did not get the same attitude from the other. In fact, when there is a rupture, it is best for everyone to go their own way because trust has been broken. And when trust is broken, there's no way to mend it.

If someone complains in a relationship, it's a sign that they're falling apart

Rethink your relationship if your partner shows signs that they are dissatisfied. Why stay in a relationship that's bad for both of you? Life is too short to get attached to little things. So it's best to make a definitive decision and go about your life with peace and quiet.

The world is not like it used to be, where women were married to men by social convention. The world is not like it used to be, where women depended solely on their partners to survive. The world is not like it used to be, where everyone lived by appearance to please others. We are living in a new time in which we discover self-love and strengthen our personal relationships. Being happy is more than an obligation in today's times.

Why do you reject your husband?

When a woman rejects her husband several times, she runs the risk of destroying her own relationship. If you don't want your husband, why stay with him and subject him to humiliation? Better to separate and find someone else you're interested in.

When the husband feels rejected, he goes outside to look for what he does not have at home. And there's no point in complaining about betrayal in this case. It was you yourself who provoked this situation. Be aware and change your attitude towards your husband if you really want to stay married.

But if you reject your husband for the sake of being hot, that's a bad psychological game. It's a difficult and cruel move that can wipe out your pretensions. Remember that there are millions of temptations out there out to hook your husband. Open your eyes, woman, don't reject your husband anymore.

How bad it is to date someone who corrects you all the time

If your partner corrects you repeatedly or all the time, it's a toxic relationship. It really torments you and embarrasses you in public. So it's time to finish this for your own good. Remember that it's better to be alone than to have someone tormenting you all the time.

Date someone who supports and loves you. Date someone who understands you and gives you good gifts full of meaning. Date someone who stands up for you, even if you're not completely right. To love is to truly care for the other without expecting anything in return.

The man who does not keep his promises is not to be trusted

A promise is a debt. When we make a promise and don't keep it, we lose all our credibility. So the man without credibility has no respect from anyone. If you can't deliver on something, then don't promise. Better that than being embarrassed in front of society. A man's word is a very important thing.

Don't trust a man who doesn't have a word. When you least expect it, you'll be disappointed with it absurdly. Analyze the man by his family history, society history, life history. Only then to have confidence that he is a good person. Just so to feel at ease and proceed with the project. Good luck to you.

When you dispense with leisure, it's easy to save money

If you want to achieve a dream: house, land, apartment, car, but you don't save, you never get there. For most Brazilians, buying a home is a big challenge. But if you save well, you can achieve this big goal.

Our first goal is to have a home of your own as it is your security. Then, we tried to buy a car to make it easier to get around. Too bad I was never able to buy any property with my salary. I've always spent a lot and there wasn't enough left over for me to buy a house or car. Well, I don't have a car and I live in an inheritance house. I am grateful for the work of my parents so that today I have a roof over my head.

To be able to work in a company, the employee has to have team spirit

A good employee is understanding, hardworking, assiduous, generous, knows how to work in a team and knows how to find solutions to problems. A good employee can become a boss, but without the pretense of bringing anyone down or excluding anyone. A good boss knows how to listen to every demand that comes to him at the counter.

Even if you have a higher position, don't use your power for your own benefit. Consider yourself equal to the other employees. Know how to help others so that they grow in wisdom, joy, justice and charity. Play the role of boss and employee. Know how to be understanding with everyone. It is for his good role that society admires him. It is for your good work that everyone loves you and wishes you long life.

To be a good worker, you need to be okay with yourself

Whatever we do in life, we have to have emotional stability. So if you find yourself confused, how are you going to produce significantly well? It is necessary to be up to date with emotional therapy, to have fewer problems, to be able to understand the diversities of the world, to put oneself in the other's shoes, to give opportunities to other people.

Good work is done by emotionally rich people. Good work is done by people who aren't afraid to work. Good work is done by competent and qualified people. Good work is done by people with a full spirit. Good work is work that pays the worker well. So, the work in our lives is very important but we have to follow some rules to get along.

I lived a great dark night, where I forgot about God, about his principles and only committed sins. I was the guy who liked to show my ass as a teenager and that makes me ashamed to this day. But then I reflected and saw that it was wrong. I became a better human being, more ethical, honest and kind to people. I became an exemplary son and made my parents proud.

What do we learn from the dark nights of our lives? We learn that sin is learning, but that without making mistakes, we can't learn anything meaningful. From adolescence, we live experiences that add a lot to us and make us experienced people. Today, I know I'm on the right track. My life is still full of great challenges: one of them is to make a living from my art. But even though I don't make a living from writing, I feel that what I say in books is important and should be cataloged for future generations. I take pride in literary work and consider it one of the largest literary collections in the world. So I ask that anyone who wants to support me, I will love your interest very much.

Is having many relationships a sign of love happiness?

Not always. Sometimes a person like this doesn't really have self-respect. He is a person full of neediness and self-affirmation. So she mends those relationships to make ends meet their affective neediness. Does that solve her problem? Not necessarily. This is even worse. What a person needs to develop is his self-love, love for God, and love for his neighbor.

When we have love for ourselves, we have more patience and care for those we relate to. Having a boyfriend entails many philosophical and personal issues that we are sometimes not prepared to face. So it destroys us little by little, with no chance for our savior rationalism. Thinking does a lot of good before anything else.

Why don't relationships last forever?

A new relationship is good to enjoy. Everything is new in a relationship until about three years old. But as time passes, the relationship frays and sometimes spouses seek adventures outside of marriage. That's why I say that every relationship has its expiration date these days. Nothing is really forever.

Understanding that the relationship is over is a great virtue. Maybe a change in your life will bring you more benefits and you will find in a new partner what you have been waiting for. It's always time to start over and renew expectations. We are all walking metamorphoses like caterpillars.

Dutchman's Stone

Godlike

What do you like to do most besides work?

Dutch

Work bores me. So, I come to bathe in the river.

Beatriz

But isn't skipping work a bad thing? Is this a decent man's thing?

Dutch

I work only what is necessary. When it bothers me, I come to the river and go down towards the rock.

Spirit of the mountain

What do you feel in the river?

Dutch

I feel totally connected to nature. I see that clay pits is my home. Even though my ancestors are gone, I am still grateful for the opportunity to stay here. I love all that God has provided for me.

Renato

I get it right, dear. We are young and we have this keen perception of nature. Let's go ahead. May you enjoy your leisure well. Working is good, but not so much.

Godlike

What do you think about the future?

Dutch

I want to immortalize my name in the history of Clay pits. I want to be remembered as the Dutchman of the stone, a folkloric character. Leaving a mark on the world is what I want the most.

Godlike

Go ahead, buddy. All the best to you. May you persist in your goal and reach. This place has an indescribable culture, which moves us a lot. Long live clay pits!

'   Thus, was immortalized the history of the Dutchman's stone in Clay pits. A remarkable character from the colonial time when the Dutch dominated the state of Pernambuco.

Godlike

Why are you screaming, young lady?

Girl

I lost everything a girl could have: her family, her shame, her reputation. Everything seems cloudy to me.

Beatriz

Don't give up, young lady. All of us women have our magic and enchantment. Don't let depression overwhelm you like that. You have so much to provide to all of us.

Girl

It's very difficult to control this revolt that I feel. Why are we so punished by men? Why do we have this role of submission? Why is it that when something goes wrong it's our fault? I wanted to experience freedom and less daily pressure. It seems like that's so much to ask.

Spirit of the mountain

You have your personal worth. Believe in yourself and don't mind the criticism. Be the simple woman you've always been and awaken your inner glow. Women from the interior of Pernambuco have a lot of value.

Girl

I understand my worth, but I still feel sad. I want to depart from this world as a form of protest. I want to shut the critics' mouths and mark history.

Renato

Don't kill yourself! Think what's best for yourself. Life is too beautiful to be wasted. React!

Girl

I've already done my part. But society is pretty cruel. Because of a mistake of mine, I was judged and condemned a lot. I thank you for the strength you give me, but no one understands what I feel. What good is life without honor? I answer myself: nothing!

Godlike

Follow your destiny, dear girl. But know that we love you no matter what decision you make. You are part of the culture of clay pits and will forever be eternalized in our hearts. May God bless you.

At night, the girl committed suicide on the beach of Clay pits. Legend has it that locals hear screams of anguish coming from the beach on full moon nights. She met her fate, but too bad it was so painful for everyone. In her honor, the stone she died on is called the girl's stone.

The Horse Graveyard

Godlike

Are you sure you want to sacrifice that poor horse?

Foreman

He has cancer. He is sentenced to death. Let's cut short your suffering.

Renato

See how he suffers. It looks like it doesn't want to die. Mercy. Is that really necessary?

Foreman

It's hard for me too, but it's the best for him too. At least, the suffering is temporary.

Beatriz

Horses also have feelings and soul. Do they love their owners and get it in return? What tyranny.

Foreman

He is an animal that helped me a lot but is unable to do so due to illness. I'm trying to help you.

Mountain spirit

His spirit will suffer greatly due to loving his owner. The body seems to resist the wounds. He suffers but refuses to die. He feels exhausted, sick, but looks like he's still standing.

Foreman

That's the hardest horse to die for. So I'm going to rush the process. He has to rest in peace to forget this worldly life of suffering. Go in peace, Lipe, we'll meet in heaven.

With one more well-aimed blow, the horse finally falls. Everyone present mourns the loss of the animal that was loved by everyone in Clay pits. It goes down in history as a folkloric legend of the city. The horse is gone, but the spirit remains haunting the place for all eternity.

Why do many artists regret being famous?

I think the main reason you regret being famous is the exposure on the internet. When we have our personal life exposed, we see that being famous has advantages and disadvantages. So, by being famous, we have an easy time making dreams come true and getting financial advantages. But we also expose ourselves more, letting many know about our lives. This can be exciting, or it can also be uncool.

Personally, I prefer a simple life. I prefer my life on the farm, where I have peace, tranquility and harmony. But it is quite true that not being famous brings financial and market losses. I can't, for example, make a living from literature because almost no one knows my work. I also can't be part of digital media or even be reported in the press. That's a disadvantage of not being famous. But I am happy in my poverty and in my anonymity.

Why shouldn't we be afraid?

Fear imprisons us. Fear causes us to channel negative energies. So fear gets in the way of our lives a lot. If we're not afraid, we're going to face problems head-on and we're going to overcome anything. Even if the answer is a betrayal, a rejection, or a death. We will live with the pain and the loss, but we will be able to overcome it.

Have the courage to live your life. Have the courage to make the right decisions. Have the courage and faith to wait for the right moment. Have the courage to be who you are. Don't wear any masks about yourself or your sexuality. The good ones and those who like you will support you. So those who rejected you were just leftovers. Remnants of a past you won't remember. You are more important than all of them.

We are complete people. So avoid the lack

Feeling fragile, dependent, and needy can get in the way of your relationship. Learn to love yourself, to value yourself, and to be a complete person. Be happy for yourself without depending on others. When you reach that point of balance, you will be ready to live any relationship.

When the other is just a complement, this is an ideal relationship. Be financially and psychologically independent. If everything goes wrong and the other person abandons you, you will have your own salvation. You'll be able to get over the loss quickly because you'll be a complete orange. So feel happy to be who you are, with a lot of love for yourself.

Did you know that death is inevitable?

We don't like to think about it. But the truth is that the only great certainty we have in life is death. Death is the fate of all that is alive on earth. And how to face this reality? Enjoying each day of life intensely. Forgive, love, be generous, be charitable, change jobs, travel a little, cheer yourself up even if you're facing depression. You are valuable and you have to love yourself first and foremost.

Don't think about death. Live every moment of your life with the joy that is eternal. Do good while you can so that you leave good memories in those who love you. Make every moment count and don't have too many worries. Worries, fear, and shame enclose our souls in a fetid environment. So leave your soul free to provide yourself with the best in life.

Thinking about death is depressing. But if it weren't for death, we wouldn't have life. Everything has to have an ending so that other people can have a chance to live on earth. Therefore, there is no one irreplaceable. The next day, they are replaced and life goes on. All the material you had is donated or inherited. Everything you were jealous of and didn't want to lend will end up in other hands. In a few years, you are forgotten by most people. Myself, I don't have children. So my gift to the world will be my books that will remain for posterity. That's why I take this writer's job so seriously. I ask readers to support me so that I can continue to produce more and more content.

What do you think of old age?

Old age is something that will come for some people. Others will not reach old age because they will be dead. So how do we face old age? Face it with sobriety and animosity. Old age is the crowning achievement of a life full of stories to tell. And how good it is to reach old age with health, will and determination to win. We can conquer even big dreams and share beautiful moments of life with those we love. You are not dead yet and you can still enjoy life very well.

I see myself as old and still up to some things. I will definitely be writing books because this has been my great destiny since I was a child. I will also be taking care of my farm, my animals, my family and maybe living a great true love. I have a great hope that I will be well in my old age and not depend on the help of others. I want to be a self-employed old man with the ability to do my own thing. All things are possible for those who believe in God.

I believe that in my old age I will eat of the fruit I am planting now. I will have my life stabilized, retired and with a lot of desire to live. I will still be a little dreamer, with a young mind although physically older. Age is just numbers and nothing more. What matters is that we are young at heart, with plans for the future and the present. So I will always be happy with myself, despite the great challenges I may face. Live life with joy.

Don't want to control other people's lives

Let your family, your friends, or even your partner be free. They have this right that has been given to them by God. So why try to deprive them of it? This is illegal and unfair. If you find something wrong, let us know. But never want to control anyone's life. Not even if that someone is your child.

When we are free, we have our artistic expressions preserved. When we're free, we feel free to make our own choices. Rightly or wrongly, they will build in us a warrior and winning personality. We will be experienced people, able to know what is good and what is evil. So there is no other possible way. It is by making mistakes that you learn and move forward.

I don't have my own personality yet. I've never had that from living with my family. I lived with my father, my mother, and my siblings. After my father and mother passed away, I am living with siblings. And since my siblings are older, they're the ones who run the house. I'm just a spectator of things because they don't even listen to me.

Living with family has advantages and disadvantages. The advantage is that they keep me company. The downside is not being able to have any friends or boyfriends over to your home. I understand that living with other people limits me in many things, but it's the best option for me. I don't want to be alone or helpless.

My frustration in romantic relationships has shown me that the real support I have is from family. When I needed it most, strangers didn't support me. So I'm grateful for everything I experience with my family. I am grateful to everyone who has participated in my life, family members or strangers. I have a little bit of each person in the experiences I've had. That's why I call myself the eternal learner.

How to get along well as a family

Family is the first nuclear family that we participate in from the moment we were born. It is here that we learn the basics of respect, politeness, and responsibility. It is where we learn to love unconditionally, to socialize and to have a certain worldview. Family is the beginning of everything.

Usually, when we are in danger or need, it is our family members who help us. So family has a strategic importance in the lives of all of us. It's our base of support for everything. So if you have a family, value it as a big prize.

In my forty years of life, I have to confess that those who supported me and were by my side at all times were my family members. The strangers, on the other hand, did not actively participate in any personal support for me. The few times I had contact with strangers was at school, at work, and sometimes in my own home. In other words, the times someone asked me for support was out of interest in something. But as soon as they do that, they simply disappear from my living environment. So are most people. They only look for you out of interest. After that, you fall by the wayside.

Afonso Pena and his father went to work in the fields for the first time. He was a twelve-year-old teenager studying high school while his father was a well-known farmer in the area. They were both walking side by side up the local mountain. It was a good atmosphere between them as they respected and loved each other as a family.

Afonso Pena

I'm really looking forward to it, Dad. What do you intend to teach me on this working day?

Domingos Pena

I want to teach you what the life of an honest man should be like, son. I recognize that you are a talented young man and need to study and pursue a career. But it is important that you know our origins and participate in some way in our income. I want to teach you the value of work and how to behave in front of it.

Afonso Pena

That's really important. I know that our livelihood comes from the income from the farm and the gold mine. I want to learn everything I need to about this financial issue. But first, how am I supposed to be a great man?

Domingos Pena

It must have honesty and character. You must fulfill your obligations and responsibilities. He must love and protect his family and his wife. He must work to make ends meet and keep up. It should be kind, charitable, have respect and love for others. But you should always be their priority because if you don't, no one will.

Afonso Pena

I'm beginning to understand, Dad. That interests me a lot. I will strive to be a good learner and I am sure that these teachings will be valuable for my personal development. Let's keep walking and I want to get to the tomato plantation soon.

The journey continues. In young Alfonso's mind, there were numerous questions about himself, his family, and his role in society. It was the mind of a middle-class young man, accustomed to the convenience of many things. But he needed to understand everything that was happening around him and he had his father's help to do so.

They complete a quarter of the route. The new achievement opens his eyes to the simple things of life as a beautiful sunset, the wind hitting their faces, the cicada singing, the rocks turning, in short, the pleasure of contact with nature that opened up to their eyes. He carried with him the decision to study all of this deeply.

Further on, they complete half of the route. Then they make a quick stop under a mango tree. They take the opportunity to eat some fruits and cool off.

Domingos Pena

Look at all the effort we make, son. It's the same with any venture. None of us have it easy in this world. Day after day, our routine suffocates us and shows us that work is worthy, but it is also a great paradox. Why do we work? Why do we try so hard? To make dreams come true!

Afonso Pena

My dream is to become a lawyer and a politician. And what was your dream, Dad?

Domingos Pena

My dream was to be a family man, a farmer and a miner. I got exactly what I wanted. How did I do that? With a lot of determination and hard work. Nothing is really easy.

Afonso Pena

I am one of your admirers. I am proud to be your dream child and companion. I feel that Brazil needs someone like me to change and grow. I want to perform my duties so that the Brazilian people have a better hope for better days.

Domingos Pena

I'll help you in this adaptation process. The road is long and challenging. But if you have the courage and willingness to do as you have today, we can have hope. A good son can be a good lawyer and a good politician. Ever since you were born, I feel like you're going to be a big star.

Afonso Pena

Thanks, Dad. I hope so. Let's continue with the walk. Time passes quickly.

The walk is resumed with even more energy by the two. Quickly, they overcome all the obstacles that lie ahead. In his passage through each of them, there remains this mysterious taste of good conquests, joys and victories. And it was all very new and challenging for each of them. They felt happy, with new Cheerful and ready for every challenge they faced. That's how they complete three-quarters of the route.

The last part of the route is covered with a certain tranquility. As soon as they arrive at the tomato plantation, they start inspecting the work of the employees and also helping with the tasks. It was a good activity that distracted them and brought them good fluids. There were a lot of people committed to doing their best and that was good for the success of the cause. They spend almost five hours in this job, participating in everything. At the end of the day, they feel proud of themselves and ready to assimilate everything they learned there. The next day, they would go to the gold mine to inspect the family's second venture.

In the Gold Mine

They arrive at the underground gold mine. Together with the workers, they use the machines to extract gold. Then the conversation begins.

Afonso Pena

This place is mysterious and incredible. What do you want to teach me here, Dad?

Domingos Pena

I want to teach the value of the land, natural resources and their preservation. Brazil is rich in natural resources and good management is able to preserve this condition for a long time. As a politician, you can encourage this in a special way. Look at the conditions of the mine worker. Give them their related rights, their guarantees of a lasting life, their retirement and other rights such as education and health. By respecting others, we can create wealth for all.

Afonso Pena

Now I understand everything, Dad. Your responsibilities as the head of the family are great, and I respect that. I will need your support on my path of growth and development. Thank you so much for showing me this.

Domingos Pena

No need to say thank you. I feel like I've succeeded in my goal. Now, you know where all our comfort comes from and everything we consume comes from our lands. Cherish the land, son. She has been our mother since birth. Nature is wise and we should always listen to it.

Afonso Pena

Okay, Dad. Now we can go home. I'm ready to pursue my dreams with more will. I'm sure I'm on the right track. Thank you so much for everything.

After hours at the gold mine, they return home. The little apprentice politician still had a lot of questions to do. Everything was in its own time. For now, the boy was still young and had a lot to learn.

Family Reunion

Afonso Pena finishes high school. Now, I was going to pursue a college degree. So he gathered the family to communicate this.

Afonso Pena

I'm going to move to Saint Paul. I want to go to law school and learn the laws. After that, I will become a politician and put this nation back on track. I want to thank you, my parents, for your emotional and financial support so far. I also want to thank all the employees of this farm who have always been so faithful. All of us together have great strength.

Ambrosine

I always knew I was her favorite maid. As a black woman, I ask you to fight in government for the abolition of slaves. We need our freedom in order to exist better. So I ask for your support, my dear son.

Afonso Pena

True, Ambrosine. Thank you so much for your dedication to your work and your love for me. I will engage in the struggle against slavery, against poverty and against injustices. That's why I'm going to train as a lawyer.

Ana Pena

Don't forget your parents at any point. Come and visit us on vacation. We are proud of you.

Domingos Pena

Let's hope for your success. You're ready to take on the world because you're a made boy. Go ahead, son. It's going to be all right.

Afonso Pena

Thank you all. I promise to be a righteous man and not to let you down.

Afonso packed his bags and left for Saint Paul to study. A new world was opening up for the young man who wanted so badly to succeed in life. A great luck for him.

A Debate in Law School

Rui Barbosa

What do you want to be a politician for, Alfonso?

Afonso Pena

I wanted to change the reality of Brazil, which is catastrophic. We live in a period of economic and social stagnation where no one grows. So I want to get into politics to fight against social injustices, slavery, poverty and improve the overall outlook.

Rui Barbosa

Very well. I also want to be active in politics to do my part. We need to come together to improve Brazil.

Joaquim Nabuco

We need to improve health and education, which are precarious areas. We need to stimulate the economy and create jobs. Only in this way will Brazil grow.

Castro Alves

We need to stimulate cinema, music, literature and the arts in general. The world breathes art that is a way for people to express themselves. We are going to transform Brazil into a developed country full of educated people.

Rodrigues Alves

We will found the Academic Press, to debate political, legal, educational and personal issues. We need to set up an apparatus to make this country wake up. That's why knowledge of the laws is so important.

Afonso Pena

Thank you all. College has been of paramount importance for my personal learning. We're building valuable relationships that we'll carry with us for a lifetime. We're going to change this country soon.

Afonso Pena's political career

Afonso Pena had a brilliant political career. He held the following public offices: He was a councilman and mayor of the city of Belo Horizonte. He played a large role in these positions, being distinguished by the leadership, intelligence, persuasion and advancement of the lower classes. As Minister of Justice, he contributed to the progress of the nation, using his knowledge of law to promote a less unequal and fairer country.

But his great highlight was as president of Brazil in the period from 1906 to 1909. His role was paramount in the country's development. Just as he had promised, he fought social inequalities, fought against slavery, helped poverty, generating consistent economic development.

Afonso Pena marked the country as a ruler who supported justice, health and education. This period was a period of great prosperity and change for all. For this reason, he will always be remembered as a great president.

Remember your origins

We all have a beautiful story to tell. Generally, we who are poor, start from the bottom until we study, grow up, work, and have a dignified life. Most people fight hard for their dreams and their achievements are the result of a lot of effort. So when we achieve something, something like a movie plays in our heads. It is recognizing that our conquered fruits are our great prize that life has given us.

I am proud to be homosexual, poor, from the northeast of Brazil. I pride myself on liking beggars, blacks, and women. I am proud to do charity with street children, with the poorest, to help my family and to love myself above all else. I pride myself on being an example of an undisputed human being in his virtues. So what matters most in a human being is his character, goodness and dignity. That I have in spades.

A beautiful story of overcoming challenges

Eriberto was born into a family of farmers in the interior of the state of Pernambuco. The conditions in which he was born were precarious. The financial and logistical problems were great and he had to adapt from an early age to a simple life without perks. Despite this, he lived happily in the countryside with his parents and two brothers.

Her childhood was painful. At the same time that I was studying in public school, I did small jobs. He was a farmer, a bricklayer, a construction worker, a cleaner. Anything that made him money and was worthy, he agreed. So he was learning the basics of character, honesty and working in life.

During high school and high school, his desire to study medicine grew in him. However, as his family was very poor, this dream was very difficult to fulfill. But it seems that something gave him strength and he unfolded. He struggled to study in his spare time and became a dedicated and competent student. With the prominence in school, he received more encouragement from teachers and parents who also believed in his dream. And so time went by quickly.

It's time for the college entrance exam. He signed up and prepared for three months. He took the test and waited for the result, which was positive. He was approved in the vacancies of public quotas. That was the beginning of a great journey of almost ten years with a lot of work, daily sacrifices, many financial and personal challenges. But in the end, it was all worth it. He graduated as a doctor and with his work he can help his parents and siblings. Today, he is the pride of the family and a symbol that dreams are possible. Cheers to those who believe in education.

How much maturity has changed me

I have completed my forty years of life. It has been exactly four decades of a beautiful trajectory, but full of difficulties and challenges. When I look back and see how much I've grown, I'm thankful for my maturity at the age of forty. Today I see that it was worth living each thing in my life and growing with it.

Today, I have fewer expectations in love and more rationality. But I only reached this emotional level after a lot of suffering in love rejections. There were years of misunderstanding, despair, doubt. But I came here aware that to be happy, I depend only on myself and no one else.

It wasn't easy at all. I shed rivers of tears as my tormentors laughed at me. I suffered from rejection from co-workers, schoolmates, my family. No one understands the homosexual. They say they respect it, but they walk away. They don't want any kind of contact or friendship. We are thrown out of the group just because of our sexual orientation. It's too insane and cruel a world. For this reason, the suicide rate among homosexuals is very high. We are losing our young people to prejudice.

But I have hopes. I am hopeful that the world will evolve, but I anticipate that it will not be an easy process due to the religious beliefs of the majority. As the world evolves, we will be less religious and more human. We will have more love instead of judgment. But it's a long way to go. May the new generations learn to respect their neighbors more.

The lover is the point of discord and joy. It is a person in need of affection and love who gets involved with a married person. Without going into the merits of the matter, the lover fulfills his role faithfully in the life of the couple in question. Having a lover means that marriage is no longer so interesting. Having a lover means that you want to seek outside the joy lost within a failed marriage.

I don't see the figure of a lover as a guilty figure. I don't see the lover as solely responsible for the destruction of a marriage. Perhaps the figure of a lover is the salvation of a failed marriage because once it is over, each one is free to follow his or her own destiny.

While I wouldn't blame the lover, I wouldn't be one of them either. In my mind, I've always been my priority. So being a person's second choice was never my plan. Although I don't want to be better than anyone else, I'd rather be single than have to be someone's lover. It's simply a personal choice of mine.

The Story of Two Lovers

Kitty was on the seaside at Tijuca Beach in Rio de Janeiro. Her days were peaceful, quiet, but cold and monotonous due to being a single woman for a long time. For many years, she dreamed of winning love, of having a prince charming all to herself. But the years went by and nothing concrete happened. During this period, she had fleeting relationships that did not fulfill her mood. She was alone, lost in wanderings that left her in a bubble, in the deep darkness of her soul.

Then, one night, at a bar by the beach, she met a man named Wenceslas. He was a very handsome, stunning man with honey-colored eyes, plump cheeks, tall stature, manly build, brown skin, and a captivating smile. The two began talking for many hours at a time. Right at the beginning of the conversation, they realized that they had an affinity and good chemistry between them. It was amazing just how two strangers could get along so well. They shared joys, shared personal stories, secrets, desires and goals for the future. Later that night, they exchanged phone numbers and email addresses, and added to each other on social media. It was the beginning of a promising relationship.

Kitty discovered that Wenceslas was engaged to another woman. But despite this, she couldn't resist the desire she felt to share something greater with him. That's how she became his mistress. She knew she was embarking on a difficult path. She knew she was going to be judged as a homewrecker. She knew that being a lover was like a double-edged sword. You never know what the ending would actually have. In her mind, being with him was a way to find some happiness in her life, since she never knew what it was like to have a family. She had needed to fill her emotional need for a long time, and she didn't see a better opportunity than this.

As time went by and they lived together, the relationship between the two became stronger. He was a romantic, honest, hardworking man, always treating her with great affection, respect, admiration and serenity. He surprised her with gifts on special dates, with declarations of love, and planned romantic trips to get away from the routine. Their relationship grew, and they rarely argued. For about three years, they shared special moments, in enchanting places, full of culture and history to learn. Enjoying each other's company, moments of pleasure and freedom, and creating unforgettable memories wherever they went.

At the end of a three-year period, he finally separated from his wife, and they decided to move in together. So they began, seeking a more shared life. However, they realized that what was once enchanting had become routine in their lives. The passion, the love, the attraction, just went downhill. With this, they realized that they enjoyed the time they were lovers more because they had no commitment to each other.

The question we pose is: "Is the lover a person who really destroys the happiness of others?" As they moved in together, they discovered a terrible truth, which was that marriage is not a child's dream. Maybe that's a great lesson for everyone. Perhaps they now realize that they have hurt someone and so they are reaping the law of return that never fails.

In conclusion, the story of Kitty and Wenceslas shows us that extramarital relationships can have many consequences that are difficult to digest and that not always being together is the best choice. Love, each other's companionship, and romance may be good, but being married is a totally different reality than sporadic encounters. Being a lover can destroy our self-esteem, end a marriage of many years, and yet be only moments of pleasure and nothing more. Therefore, cheating is not the best option to solve a problem in a relationship. It's best to separate, reflect, and then make big decisions. Only then will no one get hurt out of it.

Can men and women be friends?

I believe so. More than sex, People nowadays have this feeling of caring and belonging to a cause. There are people we know, who immediately feel that beautiful affection that is to be friends. Even if we are married, we can have many sincere friendships.

But this varies from person to person. There are men who are exclusively sexual and think like animals. Therefore, they take advantage of the friendship with the victim and want something more. So in this case, they always think about the sexual issue. But not all men act this way.

Want some advice? Trust men less, but let them be free. If they If they want to betray, you can't stop them. So if you really want a man's affection, let it be spontaneous and don't force anything because it's not worth begging for love from anyone.

The love between friends turned into a relationship

Cassandra and Carlos had been friends since childhood. They met in their small district of Horsefly, in the state of Pernambuco, and quickly hit it off. In the beginning, their friendship was marked by common moments, great adventures, great stories, and an affinity and understanding that were very good. However, their different commitments, their lives themselves, their different social classes kept them just as good friends, even though they had a beautiful feeling for each other.

When they finished high school, Cassandra and Carlos moved to another city, but promised to keep in touch. They communicated by letter, phone calls, e-mails, and thus killed some of his longing. There were long years of despair for not sharing the same physical space anymore. But they still dreamed of more things.

Five years later, they met again on the feast of the patron saint of Horsefly, Saint Theresa. It was a special night, with lots of dancing, music, religiosity and love. They stayed together and thus began a relationship.

From then on, they found themselves with more frequency. After two years of dating, they got engaged. And a year later, they got married. Really, they were sure they wanted to be together forever. They had three children: two boys and a girl. Their love was complete in the small things and in the big ones as well. They were moments of happiness, but also of sadness and disappointment. And so they stayed together for twenty years.

Carlos He passed away, but the good memories remained. Everything they built together was their life testimony. Yes, it is possible to build a marriage on friendship. Even if life shows us several twists and turns, those who love each other end up together because love is greater than everything. How beautiful true love is and its examples give us the strength to continue fighting for our own happiness.

There are men who live double lives

There are men who have two marriages at the same time and sometimes manage to hide it for a long time. They are the so-called polygamous men. Without going into the merits of the ethics of the issue, I can say that this double life is a great farce and can bring financial and psychological damage to individuals.

Polygamy is just one way of looking at the world. It's a way of living that contradicts the rules we were raised with. But for some people, it's no mistake or sin. So let's stop judging and understand that this is a different way of looking at the world. However, no one is obliged to accept to live a farce. So there are people who break up when they discover this fraud.

Don't be depressed

Are you very sad? Are you tired of your routine and everything around you? Do you feel anxious and thinking about the future? See a psychiatrist. It could be stress or the onset of depression. Investigating as soon as possible will give you a chance to recover as soon as possible.

Being sad and unfeeling at times is normal. What's not normal is if the symptoms persist. So be careful and watch yourself for a while. Our health will always come first. Nothing is more important than our health: no money, no work, no achievements. God and health are the pillars of our life.

My personal story as an example of overcoming challenges

Dear fellow writers and readers, I am here to give my personal testimony that can also serve as an encouragement for many who are still at the beginning of the literary path. My dream in literature began at a very young age, in my adolescence. The Possidônio Tenório de Brito Foundation opened a good library in my community and divided my time in school, working in the fields and reading, I spent my days. I've lost count of how many book collections I've devoured in this time. Being a reader was really good, but I wanted more. I grew up in this world of healthy dreams. Already in adulthood, in 2006, when a relatively serious health problem weakened me to the point that I felt inadequate, literature was an escape valve so that I could gradually free myself from my inner demons. At this time, I wrote a small book on a few scratch sheets. At that time, it was unthinkable for me to have a computer due to my unfavorable conditions. That wasn't my moment. I saved my drafts for a later date. In 2007, I started typing my book in between at work, saving it on a floppy disk. I was so unlucky that the floppy disk burned out. I started the degree course in Mathematics and once again I left my dream aside. I finished college in 2010 and the following year I bought my first laptop. By this time, I had already written my first novel and prioritized its typing. I released it that same year. I had fulfilled my dream of being a published author, even though my financial situation was still catastrophic. I stopped again with my dream. At the moment when I no longer expected it, I passed a public exam and resumed literature at the end of 2013. Just feeling the pleasure of readers from my country and other countries reading my writings was worth all my effort. My goal in literature goes beyond money, as income I have my job. It's sharing concepts, transforming and creating new worlds, it's touching people and making them more human in a culture of peace. It's believing that even facing the normal toil, problems that everyone has, I can dream of better days. Literature has completely transformed me and everyone around me. I owe everything to my great God who always supports me. I will continue my journey with faith in my heart and immortalizing this gift of God forever. Therefore, my dear colleagues, never give up on your dreams. You can do it!

Currently, it's been ten years since I've resumed writing continuously. I have written fifty books and am published independently in more than thirty languages. Even if I haven't achieved literary success yet, for me I'm already a great success. I am successful for being this warrior man willing to do anything to survive and provide for his family. I am a success because I believe in my art and the power of the word. In these seventeen years of literary career, I can proudly say that I have survived. I have survived all the challenges that life has thrown at me. I continue to believe in my talent and continue with a lot of energy with my literary works. I'm proud of every book I've written because each one has valuable lessons. I am proud to be an advocate for the LGBT group, to fight against racism, to fight against prejudice, to defend the poor, the street child, the orphan and the marginalized. I pride myself on being an honest, generous, and charitable man to others. The world would be so much better if everyone shared my ideals of justice, equality, and love for all.

Are you tired of your family, your friends, your wife, your parents or your partner, who don't support you in your dreams? I have a big question for you: Don't expect support from anyone. To make your dream come true, you need: planning, action, money, and a lot of goodwill. You can just go further even alone on your way.

Your faith and hope can make up for this lack of support from others. And then you'll be happy to take every step that life throws at you. Believe in God, in yourself, and in your talent. You can and are able to overcome all difficulties. Don't believe your opponents who disqualify your work.

If you're going to listen to other people's opinions, you're never more than just a failure. React and show all of them your great problem-solving skills. Then you will find in yourself the happiness you have been looking for all your life. Cheer up and go for it.

The Little Gymnast

Marcélia was a beautiful young woman who lived in the countryside of Piauí, born into a very poor and humble family. From childhood, she demonstrated tremendous strength and a phenomenal willingness to face the common problems of routine. While several children in the same age group didn't worry too much about the future, she was engaged in each of her dreams. We can say that she saw poverty as the fuel to want to win and change that reality.

His childhood was not easy at all. His time was divided between school, working in the fields and playing sports. As a child, you could see that she was a young woman full of talent. But winning would not be easy at all due to his precarious financial condition. The days in the fields were miserable. He battled in the fierce sun, without rest and without luxuries. What gave her the strength to fight was her dream of being a professional sportswoman, a renowned gymnast. And so his days were spent in great difficulty.

In her childhood and adolescence, the lack of support was glaring. Not even the family believed in his dreams. But the girl was there, training, insisting on a dream that only she herself believed in. For this reason, many people had a special admiration for her.

Upon graduating from high school, she made a difficult decision. He left his family and moved to the city of Saint Paul. There, he immediately got a scholarship, and began training exhaustively. Just when she felt ready, she participated in several tournaments and got many prizes. She became the gold medalist at the Olympics, surprising everyone. Her example shows us that a dream it is possible when we strive to do it. That's why I say: never give up on your dreams, no matter how crazy they may seem.

Don't play hard in a relationship

Take it easy on a relationship, but don't play hard either. The way the world is going, you're going to lose your boyfriend to a more liberal person. Nowadays, boyfriends have sex and that's not out of this world. So why go against the odds? The risk is very high.

We have to give our best to our boyfriend. Just as we give, we also receive. So this exchange of loving energy does us a lot of good and strengthens our spirit and spirit. Well, take advantage of this dating moment to enjoy the best of each of you as a couple. It's a period that passes quickly, but it's a time of growth, learning, and love together.

To be mature is to take random conversations for granted

Maturity teaches us that conversations are important. This dialogue has to be built daily and with value. Distorted or unimportant conversations are behind us. We start to value it more to the content, the quality and the people. We start to value what really matters.

At the age of forty, everything has a special flavor to me. Practically middle-aged, I am a mature person, aware of my duties and obligations to society. This shouldn't suffocate me, but it does alert me to potential scams. So I go about my life with a lot of care and appreciation for my life.

Well, being mature invites us to intuitive reflection. What do we do? Where are we going? Where did we come from? Only in yourself do you find these enlightening answers. So let's dive into that inner sea of emotions and feel that unparalleled taste of personal achievements that we can get. It's all worth it, you just have to believe.

Someone very close to you betrayed you, deceived you, and despised you. Is it possible to forgive? Is it possible when the one you trust the most has set a trap for you and discriminated against you for your way of being and seeing the world?

There is a process of grief necessary for him to recover from the psychological blow to which he has been subjected. However, it is necessary to reflect and question oneself. Do I have any guilt in what happened? Didn't I expect too much from the other? Is it possible to give yourself a second chance? After these considerations, everything will become clearer to you and you will have a path to follow.

My best advice to anyone who has experienced this kind of frustration is to give it time. As an old saying goes, time heals everything. Wait for the time of storm and wrath to pass. Focus your efforts on dispelling from your mind the emotions that harm you: hatred, revenge, guilt, and intolerance.

It is important to remember that the grudge provoked by the other will remain until you make a decision: to erase the fact (even without forgetting it) and to move on with your life (to value yourself more).

Forgiveness: This is the name of the relief of your conscience, it is what will free your heart from all sorrows and sufferings. To forgive is to rid yourself of the poison and fire that consumes your trust in others. It is not just an attitude, it is a choice of life of the soul because those who do not forgive also do not have credits that deserve God's forgiveness. But are you really willing to forgive? Sincerity with yourself is the first step in being able to forgive someone.

Jesus' forgiveness of the prostitute

Do you forgive your neighbor? Do you forgive yourself? Do you ask God for forgiveness? Do you always exercise forgiveness? If you answered yes to all of these questions, you're on the right track.

Forgiveness frees us from the poison we carry. Forgiveness frees us from hurt and hatred. Forgiveness brings us indescribable peace. So, let's follow the example of the master who forgave the prostitute. Who are we to judge others? We have our own faults to take care of. We have our own problems to solve. So, understanding others is part of the forgiveness that we continually exercise.

When I forgave my enemies, my life improved a lot. I got rid of every bad feeling that flooded my soul. I became a more joyful, more participative, more fulfilled person. I became the key to my own happiness. Today, with forty years lived, I am in a good phase, with a lot of peace and harmony. I hope that the future holds more happiness and achievements.

We've got to learn to like ourselves

My dark night of the soul was in the period of twenty years up to thirty-five years. I didn't love myself, I was looking for the meaning of life, I was looking for happiness in other people. And it was a period of great stumbling, pain, and disappointment. That's when I woke up to life.

After that, about five years ago, I ruled out the possibility of finding love. After so many rejections and so much suffering, I had the only option to value myself. Today, with forty years lived, I feel I made my best choice. I don't expect anything else from others. I can live my life alone, with great freedom. I love myself, I love God, and I feel good about myself. But this process of emotional maturation was not easy at all.

I understand that you can suffer a lot from loneliness, from your existential crises, from your anxiety, from your perspective of the future. Being alone is a big life scam, but it can be enjoyable too. We have to understand that Prince Charming doesn't exist. We have to understand: a fairy tale is good to listen to, but it only stays in the realm of ideas. We have to see that real life is totally different from the life of romance in movies and books. And it is precisely art that makes us survive the days of anguish. What would life be without art? It would be an endless emptiness.

Am I happy in my existential solitude? Yes, certainly. I am in very good health, with a lot of joy, with a lot of happiness, with a lot of energy. I've learned to make my day my best and things are always getting better for me. Being happy is my only option and I believe I'm on the right track. May God bless all my projects and may I be very happy.

Don't judge anyone in your personal battle

We all have our story and our personal battle. Judging is easy, but living what we live, only those who are in the skin. I myself have had big issues to solve throughout my life. I myself had to cry a lot to understand all the outrages I was subjected to. I've been a guinea pig in several jobs, but I haven't been happy in any of them.

Who is rich? Rich are those who do not depend on employment. Rico has his own economy and could live off his money for the rest of his life. Reality of the few and envy of the many. Who doesn't want their financial independence? But unfortunately, achieving the long-awaited independence is not easy at all. Only if you're a famous businessman.

I love being poor. I love being a writer and having good stories to tell. I love being the person I am. From a young age, I learned the good things in life. From a young age, I learned to be honest. From a young age, I learned to do good. Ever since I was little, I've had love in my heart. And so I have been transforming the lives of millions of people.

That's why I don't judge anyone. In fact, I don't even speak ill of people. If I can't help, I don't get in the way either. I do it this way because I believe in the law of return that is for everyone. Sow good today and reap success tomorrow. Plant Good Seeds Today, Water Properly and see it bear fruit. Only you will know how important it is to have your achievements that didn't fall from the sky. Only you will know what victory will taste like after waiting so long. Only you will know where the callus tightens. So, celebrate your personal success a lot and may more and more victories come.

What does God require of us?

God does not require of us any great sacrifice. Only that we be good disciples of the good. When we know that what we are doing is right, then our conscience is clearer. How good it is to be at peace with yourself and have emotional control of things. Being a leader of oneself requires brave and definitive attitudes. Being a protagonist of your story requires a love and quality of the individual's own. Are you writing your story the right way?

What do you require of yourself? And what do you do to be happy every day? The answer to these questions can give you a right direction in life. When we understand our worth, when we are able to fight for ourselves, when the love within us blossoms, we will be ready for the next step.

What does life expect from you? You have been taking care of your spirituality and the way you Do you face your obstacles? Understanding every step of our lives is important for us to plan for our future. What we can't do is lose faith in God, faith in life, and faith in ourselves. Faith is what will move mountains and perform miracles.

Faith and Hope

These are important virtues to keep alive the chance to win and progress, to make dreams come true. Every project initially represents only a desire, a goal to be achieved. The next step is to fight to accomplish it. At this moment, one must not give up in the face of stumbling blocks and obstacles, but start again with courage and hope.

Hope is a breath of fresh air for the spirit, it is longing for the help of fate, it is gathering strength. Not passive hope, but the rise in action, cooperation and organization. When you reach this stage, you need to have faith. Believe that anything is possible, have confidence. Faith is the quality that differentiates the winner from the loser, the believer from the unbeliever, the believer from the unbeliever, the fool from the foolish, the righteous from the unrighteous.

To have faith is to glimpse the future in the present, it is to feel a reality invisible to others, it is to accept and participate in the creator's project. Faith opens the doors of healing (of body and soul), shakes and removes the foundations of unbelief, frees the spirit (from evil oppression and negative currents of thought).

Therefore, faith and hope complement each other and form within us a force that transforms our lives and our relationship with God.

To be romantic is to be polite, kind, gentlemanly. To be romantic is to give yourself for real in a relationship. However, not everyone likes a romantic man. So here's a piece of advice for free: truly be what you are. If you don't please others, patience. At least, please yourself.

I am a mixture of a romantic and a pragmatic person. I am the mixture of the modern and the ancient. I am the mixture of care and freedom. So, I'm a balance between the rational and the sentimental. Not whether that is the right thing to do, but that is what I propose to do.

Being romantic isn't always ideal in today's relationships. I think romanticism is more of a thing of the past. So let's live real life today and see what our real possibilities are. Let's be happy immediately before time passes at once and takes us away. Life goes by too fast. Life is too important for us to lose in.

Final

Milton Keynes UK
Ingram Content Group UK Ltd.
UKHW040719201123
432908UK00002B/502